POLE

ARTIC CIRCLE

NORTH AMERICA

NORTH
ATLANTIC
OCEAN

HAWAIIAN ISLANDS

PACIFIC OCEAN

SOUTH AMERICA

TAHITI

NEW ZEALAND

ANTARCTIC CIRCLE

NTARCTICA

D0603915

CAPTAIN COOK

Great Names

CAPTAIN COOK

Mason Crest Publishers

Philadelphia

James Cook was an English explorer who lived more than 200 years ago. He was the greatest sailor of his time and one of the most famous sea captains in history. He sailed the Pacific Ocean three times, discovering and charting its islands, and more or less completing the map of the world. Cook was also the first European to visit Hawaii and the first European to sail along the eastern coast of Australia.

Everyone calls him Captain Cook.

Captain Cook was born near the English port of Whitby in 1728. His family was not well-off, and so when he finished school he began work in a grocer's. Then at 18, he boarded a merchant ship and went to sea to learn to be a sailor.

The captain on board his first ship, Captain Walker, was very impressed with young Cook. He said, "This boy is smart and quick. With a little more experience, he will become a top-class navigator."

For the next 10 years, Cook sailed the stormy North Sea to Scandinavia. His record was excellent, and he was frequently promoted. However, he did not want to remain on merchant ships and left to join the Royal Navy. In the navy, his skills as a navigator were quickly recognized, and by age 32 he had already risen to the rank of captain.

After entering the Royal Navy, Captain Cook was sent to survey and chart the Canadian coastline. During this trip he mastered the use of navigational instruments and realized how important science was to sailing. His later expeditions all made great use of science.

In 1767, the English government sponsored a scientific expedition to the Pacific to make an observation of an astronomical event called the Transit of Venus and search for the great southern continent, *Terra Australis Incognita.*

The English astronomer Edmond Halley calculated that Venus would pass across the face of the sun on June 3, 1769. This rare event occurs only twice, eight years apart, approximately every century. The event was important because measurements made at the transit would enable scientists to calculate the distance between the sun and the earth. Many scientists had attempted to observe the 1761 transit, but all had failed, so Halley suggested that a team be sent to a place where the event could be observed clearly. That place was Tahiti. It would be the first stop of the voyage.

To lead the expedition, they wanted an experienced captain. They chose Captain Cook.

For a long sea voyage, it is vital to have the right ship. Cook chose a Whitby collier, refitted it, and named it the *Endeavour.* Whitby is a small port in the north of England and most of the ships that traveled there were "colliers," the name for ships that carried coal to London. Although the *Endeavour* was only 66 feet (30 meters) long, it was solid and there was plenty of room below deck to stow all the food and water Cook and his crew would need.

Soon planning was complete and on August 26, 1768, the *Endeavour* set sail. On board were nearly 100 men, among them astronomers, botanists,

Quarter Deck   Main Deck

Main
Hatch

Plans of His Majestys Barke
Endeavour as fitted at Deptford
in July 1768

Great Cabin   Captains
Bedplace   Boatswains
Cabin   Gunners
Cabin with
Births   Pantry   Foremast Mast

Lobby

Mr Banks
Bedplace   Mr Surgeons
Cabin   Draughtsmen
Cabin   Pantry

Lower Decks

Mr Greens
Cabin   Surgeon   Steward   Sails
Room   Bread
Cabin   Bread

Aftr
Hold   Main
Hatch   WT

Master   2d Mate   Capt   Gunpowder
Cabin   Carpenters
Steward

Admiral
Room   Sun

Captain
Staterooms   Major

naturalists, and painters. It was to be an expedition that united science and exploration.

The *Endeavour* set course west across the Atlantic to America, then down the coast of Brazil and around Cape Horn, before finally entering the Pacific.

From the ancient Greeks onward, Europeans believed there must be a large southern landmass to counterbalance that of Europe and Asia in the north. By Cook's time, no one had yet determined if there was such a continent nor where it lay.

On April 13, 1769, after almost eight months at sea, the *Endeavour* arrived in Tahiti. It was a beautiful, temperate place—springs provided plenty of fresh water, coconut palms grew abundantly, and a coral reef encircled the island. Little wonder it was known as a "Pacific Paradise."

Cook had been warned before leaving England that they might have problems with the Tahitians, and he ordered his men to use "all imaginable humanity" in dealing with them. As a result, they were able to establish friendly relations with the islanders, and the few incidents that did occur were smoothed over. They traded beads, tools, nails, and other small items with the islanders for fresh food.

The name "Pacific" was given to the Pacific Ocean by the Portuguese explorer Ferdinand Magellan. It means peaceful, which is how he found it when he sailed there in 1520.

In July, his task in Tahiti accomplished, Cook set sail to follow his orders—go south in search of *Terra Australis Incognita*.

Cook headed first for New Zealand and in October sighted land. The local Maori were not as peaceful as the Tahitians and did not like the arrival of the foreign ship. Islanders throughout the Pacific (including Tahitians and Maoris) typically used canoes, powered by oars or a sail, for traveling. They were skillful sailors and their large double canoes were capable of long inter-island voyages.

When the *Endeavor* sailed into Mercury Bay, Maoris war canoes surrounded the ship. When they tried to land, fights broke out and Cook was forced to order his men to shoot. The Tahitian priest they had on board, Tupala, was able to

communicate a little with the Maoris and later, through his efforts, the two sides were able to trade, but they never really trusted each other.

The French Impressionist painter Gauguin (1843–1903) described the Maori people as having the physiques and spirits of athletes. They also had extensive face tattoos, which were frightening to the Europeans of the time.

The *Endeavour* sailed a figure-eight course around New Zealand, charting the coastline and proving that the country was made up of two large islands, not one, as had been previously thought.

The Dutch explorer Abel Tasman sighted New Zealand in 1642 but he was unable to go closer. More than 100 years later, Cook became the first person to sail around its coasts. The charts he made were used for nearly 100 years. Once Cook had completed his chart of New Zealand, he set off on a westerly course in search of further discoveries.

The explorers, Tasman and Dampier, had been in this region before Cook, and each had sighted parts of what we now know is Australia, but nobody yet knew whether what they had seen was part of one very large island or several smaller islands. Tasman had called the land he saw New Holland.

On April 19, 1770, the *Endeavour* arrived at what was the southeast corner of Australia. Cook immediately began work. He had two important tools: a *Nautical Almanac* and a sextant. The *Nautical Almanac* was a book that gave the position of the sun and various fixed stars on each day of the year. The sextant measured the distance of the stars from the horizon. With these tools, Cook could calculate the exact position of Australia on the earth.

Cook calculated and charted as the *Endeavour* made its way north up the east coast of this newly discovered land. He claimed the area for England, naming it "New South Wales." Cook and his men often saw smoke, which indicated people lived there.

On the morning of April 28th, the *Endeavour* sailed into a bay that lies just south of today's city of Sydney. It was a sheltered, natural harbor and by midday the ship was safely anchored off the beach. People were watching their arrival

from the headlands and when Cook lowered his boats, two men ran out onto the beach, waving their spears and shouting. Although they were clearly unhappy, they did nothing more, and Cook and his crew landed without trouble. To the visitors, the native people appeared more primitive than the Tahitians or the Maoris; and as they spoke an entirely different language, Tupala was unable to communicate with them.

The visitors were excited by what they found ashore— a rich land of forests, grassland, and marshes. The land was home to an amazing number of strange animals and plants—and so Cook named the place Botany Bay. He and his crew remained there for nine days before continuing their voyage.

After leaving Botany Bay, the *Endeavour* sailed through wonderfully calm seas dotted with innumerable small islands.

But Cook was approaching unforeseen dangers. As the *Endeavour* sailed north, it came to an area of countless rocks and islets, shoals, and reefs, where disaster threatened from above and below. They had entered the Great Barrier Reef.

At sunset on June 11th, Cook spotted the first coral shoal he had ever seen. He sailed on carefully and everything seemed to be going fine, when at 11 P.M. the ship came to a jarring halt. The ship was stuck fast on the reef. Huge waves pounded it. In an attempt to save the ship, Cook ordered 50 tons of equipment to be thrown overboard. But although this made it lighter, they had to wait for the next day's high tide before, to everyone's relief, they were able to float the ship off the reef.

The damaged ship limped to the mouth of a nearby river, at a place now called Cooktown, where the crew spent almost two months making makeshift repairs, before they were able to sail on.

Cook was very concerned about the health of his crew. On long voyages, the sailors' main foods were dry or pickled items that would keep for a long time. The shortage of fresh fruit and vegetables often led to scurvy. (It was later discovered to be caused by a lack of vitamin C.) Scurvy causes spongy gums and bleeding skin and mucous membranes. Cook followed the suggestions of a naval doctor, Dr. Lind, who knew what caused the problem. Cook bought plenty of fresh supplies at each port, and insisted that aboard his ship, all sailors had to eat their ration of lemons, limes, and oranges. At first, some of the sailors were unhappy about this, but they slowly realized it was necessary.

Taking advantage of the time spent repairing the *Endeavour*, the ship's scientists continued to explore the land. On one occasion, they returned very excited. For the first time, they had seen Australia's most unique animal, the kangaroo.

Kangaroos are marsupials, meaning the mother carries her young in a pouch. There are about 266 types of marsupials in the world, including koalas, gliders, and kangaroo rats, and almost half of them live only in Australia. The kangaroo is the only one which bounds. Its powerful, long back legs are excellent for jumping and can travel over 40 miles per hour (70 km per hour.) There are over 50 kinds of kangaroo in Australia, the biggest of them, the red kangaroo, is close to six feet (2 meters) tall when standing.

One of the naturalists on the voyage was Joseph Banks. Though he was only 25 when they set out, he was rich and enthusiastic. Throughout the voyage he made detailed records and sketches of everything he saw. On his return, these were to make him very famous, even more famous for a time than Cook himself.

In July 1771, the *Endeavour* arrived back in England to a hero's welcome. Cook was promoted to commander. In scientific terms, the expedition had been a tremendous success. Not only had they observed the Transit of Venus, but they now knew much more about the peoples of

the Pacific and had made detailed records of its plants and animals. Best of all, were Cook's excellent maps, which were the most accurate ever produced and an invaluable resource to all who came after him.

Because the first voyage had been so successful, the government decided to send Cook off again, this time to sail across the southern Pacific and see if there was, as some claimed, a "Great Southern Continent" below Australia.

After his experience on the Great Barrier Reef, Cook insisted on taking two ships this time, the *Resolution* and the *Adventure*. Should anything happen to one, the second could come to its aid.

Cook prepared a list of supplies needed for the trip and presented it to the Admiralty, where it caused much surprise, for apart from the usual flour and peas, it included large quantities of some very expensive foodstuffs.

Cook had lost 35 sailors to scurvy on the first voyage. He was determined that no voyage, no matter how successful, was worth losing the lives of any of his crew.

Left to right: Captain Cook, Captain Furneaux (Captain of the *Adventure*), Omai. A Tahitian, Omai returned with Cook to England, where he was a great success in London society.

Sailors have always used stars to help them navigate. In Cook's time, they had the sextant and the *Nautical Almanac* to help them in this, but they were still unable to measure time accurately at sea and therefore could not calculate longitude (position east and west) accurately. In 1714, the Royal Navy announced a competition with prize money of £20,000 to anyone who could invent a reliable chronometer.

Although it took nearly 50 years, the prize was finally won by John Harrison, a carpenter who had taken up clock making. Cook's second voyage was made with this chronometer, and thus he was able to chart his position more accurately than anyone before.

On the
13th of July, 1772,
Cook's second expedition left
England for the South Pacific. On the 17th of
January 1773, Cook wrote in his journal, "At a quarter past 11,
we crossed the Antarctic Circle. We are undoubtedly the first and only
ship that has ever crossed that line." The next day they ran into pack-ice.

Three weeks later, the ships lost each other in thick fog, and the *Adventure*
immediately set course for New Zealand. Cook continued on long enough to

prove that what lay at the bottom of the world was a large mass of ice, quite unsuitable for humans, before he also turned toward New Zealand.

Although Cook found Antarctica unsuitable for human habitation, this did not stop the explorers. Ronald Amundsen became the first man to reach the South Pole 138 years later.

After reuniting in New Zealand, Cook's two ships set off together to explore more of the South Pacific, but in the course of the voyage the two ships were separated again. Cook traveled in a looping, counterclockwise direction, stopping at many islands along the way,

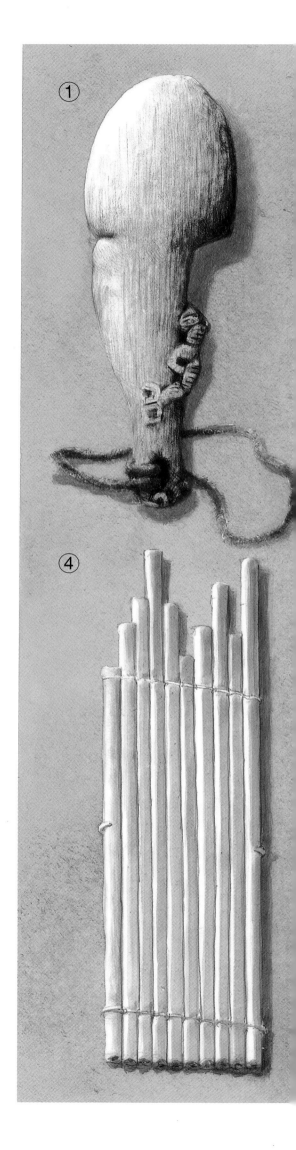

The illustrations (right) depict some of the things seen or collected during Cook's voyages around the Pacific.

1) A Maori ceremonial bone patu, or club (first voyage).

2) Spear with carved head from Malekula, New Hebrides.

3) Copy of a drawing showing one of the *Endeavour's* crew bargaining with Maoris for a lobster.

4) Reed pipes from Tonga.

5) Copy of a drawing showing Tahitian men in mourning dress (first voyage).

6) Copy of a drawing showing a crested head decoration depicting the Hawaiian war god, Ku (third voyage).

7) Ceremonial tomahawk of the Nootka Sound Indians, North America.

including Tonga, Easter Island, Tahiti, where they were welcomed back as old friends, and others. He also crossed the Antarctic Circle two more times but again saw nothing but ice.

In July 1775, Cook returned to England, having concluded, "We didn't discover the Great Southern Continent, for the simple reason that there is no Great Southern Continent. Or if there is, the waters around it are impassable. . . . Our voyage must be judged a success, however, because after facing all kinds of dreadful conditions we have returned safely."

Cook was now 46, a fellow of the Royal Society, and famous. He had discovered many new South Pacific islands and located them accurately on the map of the world. The English government now turned its attention to the North Pacific. It wanted to know if there was a passage between the north

Atlantic and the north Pacific, around the top of America. Discovery of such a passage would make the trip from England to the Pacific much shorter. Cook was asked to lead the expedition.

Cook's third voyage began in July 1776. Again he used two Whitby colliers, the *Resolution* and the *Discovery*. They sailed west around Cape Horn into the eastern Pacific, and after a long eight months, arrived in New Zealand, where they rested. Cook decided that by now it was too late to head for the north Pacific, so he lingered in Tahiti and Tonga until December 1777.

When they did head north, they discovered many more new islands, including the Hawaiian Islands, which Cook named the Sandwich Islands after his patron Lord Sandwich. He thought the people there similar to the other Pacific Islanders they had met, and he established good relations with them without difficulty.

Continuing northeast, they eventually came to the coast of America and in February 1778 anchored in Nootka Sound. They traded with the Nootka Indians for food and fur. They found,

however, that the Indians knew nothing about a Northwest Passage.

After many months of groping their way up the fog-bound Alaskan coast, Cook's ships passed through the Bering Strait and entered the Arctic Ocean. It was now August and already intensely cold. Pack-ice made progress very difficult. Having experienced similar conditions in the Antarctic Circle, it did not take them long to realize that with winter coming on, they would have to turn back.

Cook decided to return to Hawaii to repair the ships and wait for spring, when they would try again. He was greeted almost like a god on his return, possibly because of some religious prediction, but later people began to realize they had made a mistake and relations soured. Then on February 14th, one of the *Discovery*'s boats was stolen. Cook was angry and he went ashore with a party of armed sailors.

Normally, Cook was very respectful of the people in the places he visited and was careful not to offend them, but perhaps the voyage had stressed him, for this time he lost his temper.

A large crowd of armed natives had gathered on the shore, and when one of them pulled a knife and threatened Cook, Cook shot him dead. However, instead of being frightened off by this, the crowd attacked. Cook was hit on the head with a club and then stabbed repeatedly as he fell. He died on the beach, his blood staining the sands. He was 52 years old.

Despite his death, England did not forget Captain Cook's achievements; many memorials and statues were raised to him. But as one biographer said, "The best memorial we have is the maps he left us of the Pacific Ocean."

My ambition is not to go further than anyone has gone before me, but to go as far as it is possible for human beings to go.
—Captain Cook

BIOGRAPHIES

Author Richard A. Bowen resides in Wisconsin with his wife Karen. He is the editor of *Spiritual Awakenings* quarterly and co-owner of Ariadne Publishing.

Ilustrator Robert Ingpen was born in 1936 in Geelong, Australia. Ingpen's earliest work was the sketch of a shell he did when he was young. His first job, at the age of 22, was to draw illustrations and design publicity pamphlets for CSIRO, a scientific research institution. All of his illustrations were related to various scientific research reports. The work honed his perception and established his realistic style of painting. Interestingly, Ingpen's illustrations sometimes inspired scientists to explore and study the subject at hand from new perspectives. This is where the charm of Ingpen lies.

Mason Crest Publishers, Inc.
370 Reed Road
Broomall, Pennsylvania 19008
866-MCP-BOOK (toll free)

English text copyright © 2003
All rights reserved.

Illustrations copyright ©
1998 Robert Ingpen
Published in association with
Grimm Press Ltd., Taiwan

1 3 5 7 9 8 6 4 2

Library of Congress Cataloging-in-Publication Data:

on file at the Library of Congress.

ISBN 1-59084-147-6
ISBN 1-59084-133-6 (series)

NOR

EUROPE

ASIA

AFRICA

SOUTH
ATLANTIC
OCEAN

INDIAN OCEAN

AUSTRALIA

Cook's First Journey

Cook's Second Journey

Cook's Third Journey

Uncompleted Journey